THE PRESIDENT'S CAR

INTRODUCED BY FORMER FIRST LADY, BETTY FORD

NANCY WINSLOW PARKER

THOMAS Y. CROWELL
NEW YORK

Acknowledgments

The author gratefully acknowledges with thanks the assistance of Special Agent Jim Boyle of the U.S. Secret Service for information on recent presidential cars and the details attached to their operation; to the United States Secret Service for their assistance in historical background; to Mr. John A. Conde, Curator of the Transportation Collections at the Greenfield Village and Henry Ford Museum for his assistance in checking the manuscript for accuracy of historical automobiles and carriages; to Officer Lania L. Lampert, Public Information office, Government of the District of Columbia, Metropolitan Police Department, for generously researching historical photographs from their collection; and to Ms. Marcia B. Thomas, Staff Assistant, office of Intergovernmental Relations, The White House, for her interest, encouragement, and assistance in the preparation of this book.

Thomas Y. Crowell Junior Books
For information address
10 East 53rd Street, New York, N. Y. 10022.
Published simultaneously in Canada
by Fitzhenry & Whiteside Limited, Toronto.

Designed by

Ellen Weiss

Library of Congress Cataloging in Publication Data

Parker, Nancy Winslow.
The president's car.

SUMMARY: Text and illustrations present the
carriages and cars used by American presidents.
1. Presidents—United States—Transportation—
Juvenile literature. [1. Presidents—United States—
Transportation] I. Title.
E176.1.P36   1981   629.2'222   79-7898
ISBN 0-690-03963-8
ISBN 0-690-03964-6 (lib. bdg.)

1 2 3 4 5 6 7 8 9 10

Contents

Introduction by Former First Lady, Betty Ford
Going for a Ride with the President of the United States   1

George Washington   2
John Adams   4
Thomas Jefferson   5
James Madison   6
James Monroe   7
John Quincy Adams   8
Andrew Jackson   9
Martin Van Buren   10
William Henry Harrison   11
John Tyler   12
James K. Polk   13
Zachary Taylor   14
Millard Fillmore   15
Franklin Pierce   16
James Buchanan   18
Abraham Lincoln   19
Andrew Johnson   20
Ulysses S. Grant   21
Rutherford B. Hayes   22
James A. Garfield   23

Chester A. Arthur   24
Grover Cleveland   25
Benjamin Harrison   26
William McKinley   27
Theodore Roosevelt   28
William H. Taft   30
Woodrow Wilson   32
Warren G. Harding   33
Calvin Coolidge   34
Herbert C. Hoover   35
Franklin D. Roosevelt   36
Harry S Truman   38
Dwight D. Eisenhower   40
John F. Kennedy   42
Lyndon B. Johnson   44
Richard M. Nixon   46
Gerald R. Ford   48
Jimmy Carter   50
Ronald Reagan   52

Where to See Presidential Carriages and Cars   53
Glossary   56
Bibliography   58

Introduction

The president's car provides perhaps the most luxurious ride of any car in the world. Unfortunately, the president and his first lady never really get to relax and enjoy this wonderful car. They are always rushing to or from some place or event. No leisurely sightseeing around the capital for this car!

In this book you will learn about the many special features of the president's car. The very best part, however, about being given the opportunity to ride in this grand car is something on the outside of the car; something that is not even attached to the car. The best part is the people on the outside who see this car and greet it with smiles and waves for its often weary but very fortunate occupants.

— Betty Ford

Going for a Ride
with the President of the United States

When a man becomes president of the United States, he loses something most people take for granted: the freedom to jump in the car and go someplace—to the beach, the movies, the store, the office. For when the president goes out in one of the presidential limousines, the Secret Service goes over the route he will take two weeks beforehand, checks the car before he puts his foot in the door, has an agent drive the car for him, and follows his limousine with a carful of agents to insure his safety. The car is specially built, and the agents specially trained.

When the president wants an "off-the-record" trip in the car, perhaps to visit a sick friend, he tells his military aide, who in turn calls the White House usher. The usher calls the Secret Service command post for an armored car already on the grounds (at the South Grounds back door) or at the Secret Service garage. The president can be ready to roll in five minutes at night, fifteen minutes during the day.

But 150 years ago, the president was able to take a buggy ride alone around the muddy avenues of Washington, D.C., on the narrow, dimly-lit streets without any concern other than tipping over the buggy on sharp turns and having to limp back to the White House.

The presidential limousine, which the government maintains for our president's use, is the country's most impressive vehicle. This exquisitely appointed armored car, with its shrill sirens and flashing red lights, moving slowly down a wide city avenue, surrounded by armed Secret Service agents and two long lines of motorcycle policemen, is a highly visible symbol of the office of the president of the United States.

1st George Washington, 1789-1797

The first presidential carriage was a yellow-and-white, round-bottomed crane neck coach made in London and given to Martha Washington by the governor of Pennsylvania in 1777, in gratitude for General Washington's services to the country in the Revolutionary War. When he was elected president, George Washington took this carriage, known as the Penn coach, to Philadelphia, the capital at that time. He used it as the state coach on ceremonial and official occasions only, as it was too heavy and uncomfortable for long journeys.

Eighteenth century coaches were built in two basic designs—perch or crane neck. This refers to the poles supporting the carriage and resting on the axles. The "perch" was a straight or slightly bent pole under the carriage; "crane neck," two parallel iron bars bent to allow the front wheels to pass under them.

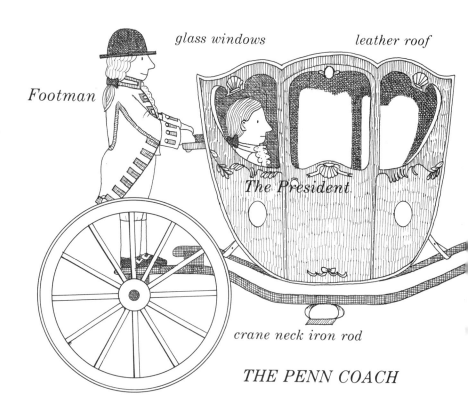

glass windows   *leather roof*

Footman

The President

crane neck iron rod

THE PENN COACH

Washington believed in upholding the dignity of his office the way the Europeans did, and thus he had the most impressive carriage, horses, and livery in the young country. His carriage was drawn by six white horses. A presidential tour included a postilion to ride a lead horse, a coachman, footman, valet, secretary, baggage wagon, driver, and a servant to lead Washington's saddle horse. On state occasions, his carriage was escorted by cavalry.

There are only two carriages of the 1700's still preserved today in the United States. One is the Powel coach, a counterpart to the coach used by George Washington, found at Mount Vernon, Virginia. The other is the Beekman coach, now at the New York Historical Society in New York City.

Only a few wooden panels survive today from the magnificent, gilded Penn coach.

off-white livery trimmed in bright orange

hammercloth of leopardskin trimmed in red and gold lace

Coachman

2nd John Adams, 1797–1801

John Adams was born in Braintree, Massachusetts Bay Colony. When he became president of the United States, he bought a carriage for $1,500 and a pair of horses to pull it, which set him back another $1,000. As the president's salary in 1797 was $25,000, this represented an investment of 10 percent of his presidential paycheck. Adams's Puritan taste reflected that of the times, when heavy, pompous coaches were on their way out and dusted off only for parades. President Adams would not agree to have the family coat of arms put on the carriage door. He abandoned George Washington's heavily ornamented coach, the guards on horseback, and the marshals.

John Adams probably drove his family from the old capital in Philadelphia to the new capital in Washington in a plain coach with crane neck poles under the carriage, a coachman on the box, and a footman holding on in the rear.

Not a splinter of wood of any of the carriages owned by John Adams survives today. The carriages were usually rattled to pieces on the old cobblestone or brick roads, and, if any survived that ordeal, public indifference to presidential carriages doomed them to rot away in fields or barns. It was not until many years later that presidential carriages and cars were lovingly preserved in museums and historical societies.

ELEGANT COACH
OF THE PERIOD

Mrs. Adams   *The President*

3rd Thomas Jefferson, 1801–1809

Thomas Jefferson was not the type to sit in a stuffy carriage and be bounced from place to place. Instead, he preferred to and did ride his favorite horse around Washington while he was president. In fact, he rode his horse to his own inauguration, the first held in Washington, D.C., and, at the end of his presidency, he rode his horse 140 miles home to Monticello, Virginia.

Because Jefferson's wife had died and there were no children in the White House, the "family carriage" was left to gather cobwebs in the barn in Washington. However, when at Monticello, Jefferson used the carriages he owned, many of which he had designed himself —chariots, phaetons, gigs, landaus, carts, and wagons.

President Jefferson was perhaps wise to ride horseback as much as he did, for carriages were cold and damp in the winter, hot and dusty in the summer, and their wheels stuck in the mud. And, they were known to tip over, completely shaking up and dumping the passengers, if not maiming them for life. As if that weren't enough, the owner of a carriage had to be rich to pay for the horses, the harness, the coachman's salary; to buy hay, straw, and oats for the horses; and to afford a stable and carriage house to put everything into.

The President-elect

5

4th James Madison, 1809–1817

The most remarkable fact about the Madison equipage is that during the War of 1812, one of the Madisons' carriages was pressed into service to save the State papers from the flames of the burning White House, set on fire by the British. Indomitable Dolley Madison, wife of the president, managed to collect the papers, stuff them into trunks and onto the carriage, and flee to safety.

The Madisons' coachee held six passengers and a driver. It was used in the city and in the country, and it had canvas blinds that rolled down to protect the passengers from rain or mosquitoes. The carriage was suspended by C springs, C-shaped metal springs at the front and back of the carriage that, over rough roads, greatly improved the comfort of the passengers and gradually replaced the crane neck and perch undercarriage designs of earlier, teeth-rattling carriages.

The Madison's best coach cost the president $1,500. It was drawn by four horses and delighted his wife. This brave, spirited woman, seventeen years younger than her husband, would dress in her most beautiful outfits and drive around the capital for all to see. She probably enjoyed riding in a presidential carriage more than any other first lady in history.

COACHEE CIRCA 1809

Dolley Madison

Coachman

C springs

5th James Monroe, 1817–1825

James Monroe was an old-fashioned man who insisted on wearing knee britches when the styles had clearly shifted to long trousers, and, just as independent-minded, he campaigned for president in a "pleasure wagon."

A pleasure wagon was a family wagon with movable seats that could convert from seating the children and aunts to hauling baggage, furniture, or sacks of grain around the rolling hills of rural early America.

Monroe's red-and-green wagon was handmade, constructed with pegs and mortised joints, for nails were in short supply. The wagon is with us today in the Shelburne Museum in Vermont.

During the War of 1812, the White House had burned down, and construction was not far enough along to put up the president and his family comfortably. So, the Monroes lived at Oak Hill, their estate in Virginia, and the president commuted on horseback to the Capital every week.

PLEASURE WAGON

length: 6 feet
width: 2 feet, 7 inches
depth: 7 inches

James Monroe

Political Supporter

7

6th John Quincy Adams, 1825–1829

On May 23, 1828, President Adams was bucked off his pony. He suffered nothing worse than a sore neck, but it was an event he thought important enough to enter in his diary, one of the most valuable records of American history preserved to date. Political observations are more prevalent in the diary than housekeeping data, and, as a result, details about the Adams carriage are slight. However, one entry tells that he did own a carriage and four horses.

As American carriage making was still in its infancy, the well-traveled Adams probably purchased his fine landau in London, while serving as minister to Great Britain, and had it shipped to the United States. The Adams carriage was described in an 1870 account as weighing 3,000 pounds, drawn by four horses, and as being a magnificent example of the carriage maker's art.

The Adams carriage survived until 1870, when it was torn up in a Cincinnati, Ohio, coachmaker's shop.

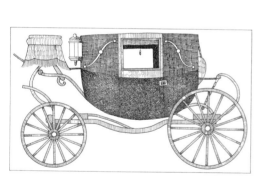

ENGLISH LANDAU CIRCA 1825

The President

7th Andrew Jackson, 1829–1837

Andrew Jackson, a former major general in the United States Army who defeated the British troops in the Battle of New Orleans, rode his white battle charger at his inauguration.

Andrew Jackson's wife, Rachel, had died one month before Jackson entered the White House. The lonely president would visit the White House stables every morning to see his favorite horse, Truxtun, named after Thomas Truxtun, commander of the U.S.S. *Constellation*.

Jackson did own a carriage while at the White House. It was Philadelphia-made, lined with red velvet, and was drawn by six white horses.

On January 30, 1835, the first assassination attempt was made on a president of the United States, but the fellow bungled the attempt, earned some blows from President Jackson's walking stick, and spent the rest of his life in an insane asylum.

The President

Truxton

STATE COACH CIRCA 1829

8th Martin Van Buren, 1837–1841

Martin Van Buren, a widower and former secretary of state in Andrew Jackson's cabinet, was a man of elegant taste. While in the White House, he owned an olive green victoria coach that was built in England and cost $1,550. Driven through the capital streets in this handsome carriage with silver-trimmed harness flashing in the sunlight, the president must have presented an unforgettable sight, dressed in his snuff-colored broadcloth coat with velvet collar, light-gray vest, orange tie, white duck trousers, morocco shoes, yellow gloves, and beaver hat.

Van Buren's victoria was a semiclosed luxury carriage with a folding roof, used for pleasure drives. It was light and could be pulled by a lighter type of horse. Its ironwork was hand forged. It had C springs and was suspended by leather through-braces. Later victorias were constructed with elliptical springs that, made of steel, revolutionized the carriage industry and surpassed the old C springs. Steel bars were concealed on both sides of the carriage body, replacing the old perch and crane neck constructions and lowering the carriage bottom so that passengers could step easily into the carriage.

Van Buren was a highly capable man, but his quick-witted political enemies took advantage of his vanity, and he was defeated in the next election.

Coachman

The President

Disapproving Whig

carriage
elliptical spring

axle →

VICTORIA CARRIAGE

9th William Henry Harrison, 1841

William Henry Harrison, the hero of the Battle of Tippecanoe, ran for president against Van Buren. Harrison ran as a man of the frontier and defeated the fashion-plate Van Buren, who could not shed his elegant image. It is ironic that Harrison was from an aristocratic Virginia family, and Van Buren of humble background.

At his inauguration, William Henry Harrison rode on a white charger in the center of seven men, all wearing plain frock coats and as alike as seven peas in a pod. But President Harrison caught cold and died one month later. He holds the grisly record of being the first president to die in office and of having the shortest presidency on record.

At the time of his death, President Harrison owned one old carriage appraised at $15 and one new carriage appraised at $500.

The President-elect and Friends

10th John Tyler, 1841–1845

John Tyler was a kind, approachable man who owned an elaborate presidential carriage. It was a rockaway, one of the most popular family carriages of the late nineteenth century, and a wise choice for the Tylers, for there were fifteen children in the family.

A Tyler descendant described the rockaway as a "black coach lined with gray broadcloth and velvet with cushioned seats and . . . two lanterns on either side of the coachman's seat. . . . It took two or four horses and . . . there was a step at the back for the footman." The rockaway was known for the projecting roof over the driver.

When Tyler's presidency was over, he and his family packed up the black rockaway and went back to their estate, Sherwood Forest, in Virginia. The estate is still occupied by descendants of President Tyler, but the rockaway was burned in a barn fire, and all that was saved were the lanterns.

Footman

Coachman

The Ex-President

Mrs. Tyler

ROCKAWAY COACH

11th James K. Polk, 1845–1849

The horses and carriages used by the president and his family while in the White House had, up to 1845, been procured on a casual basis —rich men bringing their own handsome coaches, less prosperous men accepting equipage as gifts. Even on a presidential salary, it was difficult for some to pay for a coach and four befitting the office of the presidency.

President Polk put an abrupt end to gift-giving in his administration, whether the gift came from a special interest group with strings attached or from well-meaning citizens donating an innocent present. He refused a gift horse because it was too large a present, and he used his own horses and handsome green carriage while in the White House.

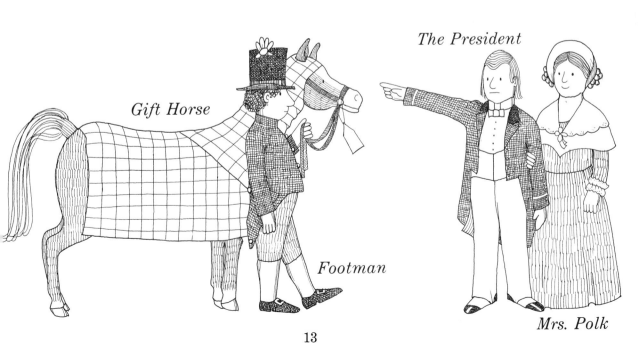

Gift Horse

Footman

The President

Mrs. Polk

12th Zachary Taylor, 1849–1850

Many of our early presidents who were fighting generals from American wars brought their beloved horses to share their glory in the White House.

Zachary Taylor was one of these men—a general in the Mexican War and the first professional soldier to be elected president. During battle, General Taylor used to sit on his horse sideways and watch troop movements. When he was elected president, he allowed Old Whitey, his famous war-horse, to graze on the White House lawn. Old Whitey's coat was long and ungroomed in retirement, and most of the hairs in his tail had been pulled out by souvenir hunters.

President Taylor also personally owned two carriages and a pair of carriage horses. He didn't get to use them much in Washington, D.C., though, for he died after one year in office, following sunstroke at the dedication ceremony of the Washington Monument. And, following military tradition, Old Whitey walked in back of the general's coffin in the funeral procession.

The President

Mrs. Taylor

Old Whitey

Richard, the President's Son

13th Millard Fillmore, 1850–1853

The Millard Fillmores had no aversion to accepting gifts while in the White House, and were delighted when the ladies of Albany, New York, presented them with a custom-made Clarence coach, and harness and horses to go with it. It was lavishly fitted inside and out, from the silver lamps on the coachman's box to the blue silk curtains on the windows. Nothing so grand had ever been built in the country before.

Millard Fillmore was one of those celebrated souls who rose from log cabin to great wealth. No doubt he enjoyed the elegant Clarence coach while in Washington, but when he became a private citizen again after his presidency, he found the carriage not suitable for his modest life-style, and so he sold it.

Coach builders were very important in the eighteenth and nineteenth centuries—the Detroit Industrialists of their time. They were in a position to contract work to large groups of workers—the wheelwrights, joiners, hammersmiths, locksmiths, saddlers, painters, and varnishers—highly skilled craftsmen in a growing industry. The finest carriages in the world came from England, and the earlier American presidents had bought their carriages in London. Consequently, the all-American carriage of President Millard Fillmore was more than a set of wheels—it was a symbol of the American carriagemaker's coming of age.

CLARENCE COACH

color: dark green
New York State coat of arms painted on door panel

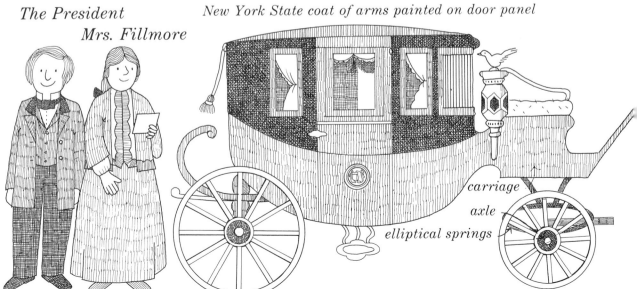

The President
Mrs. Fillmore

carriage
axle
elliptical springs

14th Franklin Pierce, 1853–1857

Two unfortunate events overshadowed Franklin Pierce's administration—the death of his young son and that of his running mate, William R. King. The grief-stricken president would often ride around the city of Washington, D.C., on his saddle horse late at night.

The kind of horse used to pull the wide variety of carriages in the eighteenth and nineteenth centuries was as important as the engine we put in different size and weight cars and trucks. The heavy carriages of the early American presidents were, by and large, pulled by two or four or even six horses. Then, as carriages became lighter and safer, two or even one horse was used. The horses, as well, varied in size. Full-sized horses pulled the heavy carriages, light horses and cobs pulled the two-seat models, and ponies pulled children's wagons on farms and country estates.

The carriage in which Pierce rode to his inauguration was a gift, made entirely of native American materials.

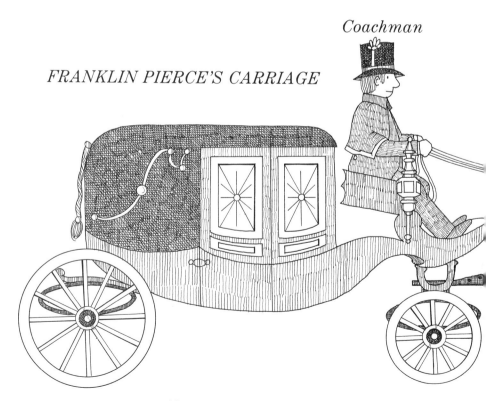

Coachman

FRANKLIN PIERCE'S CARRIAGE

The Carriage

color: maroon with a contrast of black
designed to be open or closed
axles of unbreakable gun iron
silver-plated lamps
crystal from Boston

The Horses

perfectly matched bays
16 hands high
short natural gait of 8 miles per hour

Footman   The President   Mrs. Pierce

15th James Buchanan, 1857–1861

The tall, stately bachelor president, James Buchanan, never accepted gifts. For his presidential needs, he bought a Jacobs carriage, made by S. W. Jacobs of Philadelphia, and paid a bargain price of $800 for it. With it came a fancy harness.

Although Washington winters are usually mild, it was still necessary to keep warm in the wooden carriages. Everyone used a lap robe. There were three different kinds: wool, English beaver cloth, and fur. The prices ranged from a modest $1.50 for a plain woolen robe to $12.00 for the finest California extra-fine all-wool robe, to $100 for the fur robes.

A carriage-supply-company catalog of the period lists its fur robes as follows:

Buffalo lap robes	$ 8.00–14.00
Wolf lap robes	11.00–30.00
Imitation Bear robes	11.00–20.00
Goat lap robes	6.00–8.00
Fox, Lynx, Chinchilla, Angora, Wolverine, Possum, and Skunk-	Various prices
Genuine Bear—Grizzly, Cinnamon, White, and Black Bear	30.00–100.00

JACOBS CARRIAGE

The President

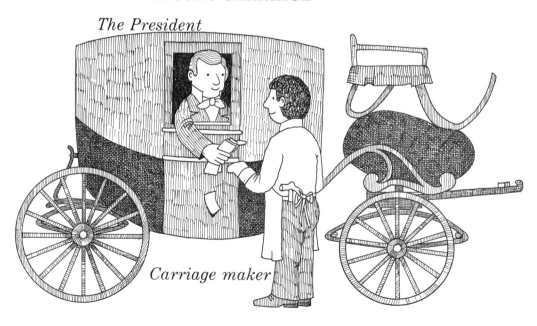

Carriage maker

16th Abraham Lincoln, 1861–1865

At his inauguration, Abraham Lincoln accepted the gift of a Brett-style barouche from a group of New York merchants. It was a silk-lined, dainty carriage with an open body, suitable for driving in fine weather.

President and Mrs. Lincoln rode in this carriage to Ford's Theater on the night the president was fatally shot. Since then, the barouche has been exhibited more than any other presidential carriage.

During the Civil War, the atmosphere surrounding the president was so charged that the Washington chief of police assigned four metropolitan policemen to guard him. There was also a Secret Service formed in 1860 as an intelligence unit for the Union Army, which was concerned over the possibility of the assassination of President Lincoln. That unit was no ancestor of the present Secret Service and was disbanded by the time of the assassination. Nevertheless, when President and Mrs. Lincoln went to Ford's Theater on April 14, 1865, to see *Our American Cousin,* there was not one policeman or soldier in the building. The man assigned to guard the president had left his post.

Despite the appalling lack of security, presidents continued to be guarded by four men from the Metropolitan Police Department until 1901, when the Secret Service took over that duty.

Coachman

BRETT STYLE BAROUCHE

length: 14 feet
width: 7 feet
height: 7 feet

The President

17th Andrew Johnson, 1865–1869

Andrew Johnson became president after the assassination of President Lincoln. He was one of the no-gift presidents, turning down a carriage and four horses offered to him by a group of New York bankers and merchants.

Instead, President Johnson brought his own carriage to the White House. The enterprising coachman was fired by President Johnson when he found out that the coachman was using the president's carriage to conduct guided tours around the capital for a profit.

Prior to and during the Civil War of Lincoln's administration and the postbellum period of President Johnson's, one-third of the money in the United States was counterfeit. This threatened the financial stability of the country. Because of this, President Johnson started the United States Secret Service on July 5, 1865, and charged its first thirty men to stop the tremendous wave of counterfeiting. This group of highly trained agents was so successful in tracking down criminals that it was only natural for it to be asked to protect the president at a later time in history.

Tourists

Coachman

CARRIAGE CIRCA 1865

18th Ulysses S. Grant, 1869–1877

When Ulysses S. Grant was president, the White House stables and carriage house were alive with activity. The restless general enjoyed horses and visited his every day—horses whose names dripped with history: Jeff Davis, Cincinnatus, Egypt, St. Louis, and Reb. President Grant liked to hitch one of his spirited horses to a light racing rig and dash around the capital at top speed. It was on one such evening's caper that the president received a speeding ticket from a D.C. policeman.

The Grant equipage boasted a carriage for every taste and occasion. After all, no self-respecting gentleman would appear at a state function hauling his family in a road wagon, a vehicle clearly designed for casual country life. There was a pony phaeton for the children, a top buggy for informal rides, a barouche for fair weather, and a landau for formal occasions.

It is hard to believe that President Grant could keep up such a fine stable, when his salary was only $25,000 per year, the same as George Washington's in 1789.

The President   *Metropolitan Policeman*

19th Rutherford B. Hayes, 1877–1881

Rutherford B. Hayes brought a brand-new four-horse Brewster landau to Washington from his estate in Fremont, Ohio. This beautiful assemblage of wood and fabric, which rattled around postbellum Washington, cost $1,150.

By choice, President Hayes served only one term in the White House. He was then succeeded in 1881 by General Garfield, who came to the White House without a carriage of his own. Such disorganization seemed out of character for this brilliant former general. Nonetheless, Hayes lent Garfield horses and carriage to use until Garfield acquired his own.

The hard-working Garfield, who had been, at thirty-one, one of the youngest brigadier generals in the Union Army, used the carriage for only five months, at which time his own arrived and he sent the Hayes equipage back to Fremont, Ohio, where it is today.

PRESIDENT HAYES'S BREWSTER LANDAU, 1877

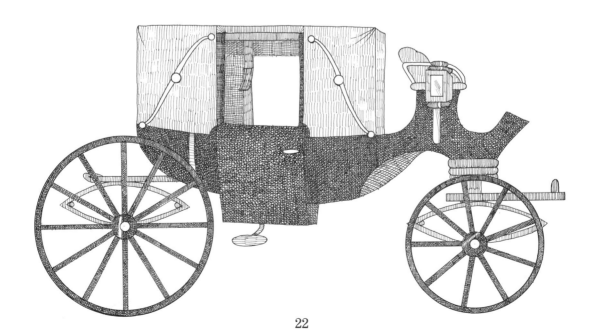

20th James A. Garfield, 1881

On July 2, 1881, President James A. Garfield was shot by an assassin after having served only six months in office, and he died two months later in the seaside town of Long Branch, New Jersey.

He had two carriages while in the White House—the one he borrowed from his predecessor Hayes and his own, which he was able to use for one month.

Perhaps the most memorable event in the Garfield presidency was the funeral given to him by his country. The hearse was a magnificent piece of Victorian funeral art, with drapery, garlands, festoons, and black-draped flags. It was pulled by twelve black horses, four abreast, whose silver-fringed black blankets almost touched the ground.

President Garfield

Ex-President Hayes

21st Chester A. Arthur, 1881–1885

Chester Arthur's landau had everything a carriage should have—glittering harness, magnificent matched horses to pull it, and, inside on the seat for winter, a luxurious, monogrammed lap robe of Labrador otter.

On taking over the presidency from the murdered Garfield, Arthur surprised his critics by being a dignified and competent president. As his wife had died one month before he took office, the saddened president would take long rides in his carriage with his daughter, Nell, beside him.

LANDAU CIRCA 1881

The President

Nell

22nd, 24th Grover Cleveland, 1885–1889 and 1893–1897

Grover Cleveland, a huge handsome bachelor when elected, was sought-after in Washington social circles, for he was the only president in United States history to be married in the White House. The president and his new first lady must have enjoyed a busy social and political life, for the carriage house contained a landau, a surrey, a brougham, a victoria, and a phaeton.

Cleveland lost to Benjamin Harrison in a bid for re-election, but came back four years later as the twenty-fourth president.

Footman

The President and Mrs. Cleveland

LANDAU CIRCA 1885

23rd Benjamin Harrison, 1889–1893

The carriage Benjamin Harrison used the most while in the White House was a simple buggy. He delighted in driving around Washington before dinner, his beard, the last ever worn by a president, flowing in the breeze. There was apparently no tight security surrounding these pleasure rides, for the president would take along his wife or niece or secretary for company. Sometimes combining business with pleasure, he would take along a cabinet member to discuss the affairs of state.

Benjamin Harrison's buggy was the most typical of American carriages. It had four light wheels and elliptical springs mounted at right angles to the traveling direction. The frame and wheels were made of light hickory cane. Manufactured in the United States, these wheels were exported and were considered the best in the world.

Besides the popular buggy, President Harrison also had a $2,000 Landau, a brougham, six matched horses, and three "office horses" —the messenger boys of the 1889 working White House.

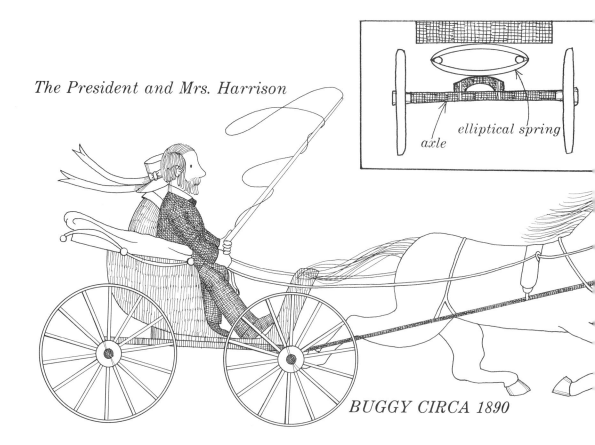

The President and Mrs. Harrison

elliptical spring

axle

BUGGY CIRCA 1890

25th William McKinley, 1897–1901

President McKinley liked to walk around the capital, or drive his own rig with his wife beside him. During his stay in the White House, he had a brougham, a cabriolet, and a landau—all rich-looking, with silver-trimmed harnesses and rubber tires. McKinley paid $5,000 for one of these monogrammed carriages. Oddly enough, this carriage fancier became the first president to ride in an automobile.

On September 6, 1901, President McKinley was assassinated in Buffalo, New York. This was the third time in 37 years that a president had been killed. The country was outraged. Every American president had been an open target, while not one ruler of England, Germany, or Spain had been killed in the previous 112 years, because those countries had strong protection for their rulers. Congress asked the Secret Service, formed to catch counterfeiters after the Civil War, to guard the president, starting immediately with Theodore Roosevelt.

WILLIAM McKINLEY'S HEARSE

carved dark mahogony wood
opens in back to admit flag-draped coffin
beveled glass on sides
silver-plated lamps
black cloth curtains

Coachmen

Military Escort

26th Theodore Roosevelt, 1901–1909

Theodore Roosevelt, at forty-two the youngest president in United States history, never used an automobile at the White House. The Secret Service, however, newly assigned to protect the president, did. When the president went anywhere in his carriage, the Secret Service followed in a 1907 White Steamer. The Steamer was manufactured by the White Sewing Machine Company, which had switched from making sewing machines to manufacturing cars. It became the second most successful maker of steam cars in the world. The White Steamers were quick-starting, safe, and easy to control.

Secret Service Agents

1907 WHITE STEAMER

The president's brougham was lacquered with so many coats of black paint that it shone like glass. The carriage body was fixed on elliptical springs and was suspended low enough to permit easy entrance. The livery of the coachman in Roosevelt's administration reflected the colors of the American flag—blue overcoat, white doeskin pants, high black boots, and a red, white, and blue cockade fixed jauntily on the side of the coachman's top hat.

In 1906, presidential protection by the Secret Service was finally enacted by Congress. In 1909, two Secret Service men were assigned officially to Theodore Roosevelt and two to president-elect Taft. This protection did not cover former presidents, and Roosevelt, campaigning in 1912 for office, was shot in the chest but miraculously recovered.

THEODORE ROOSEVELT'S BROUGHAM

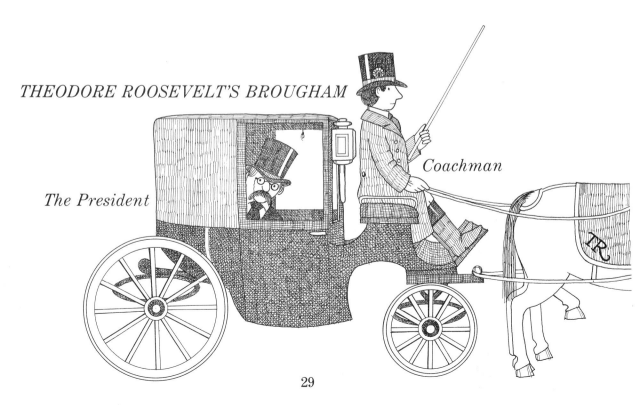

Coachman

The President

27th William H. Taft, 1909–1913

One of the most remarkable facts about President Taft is that he was the heaviest president ever in the White House. He weighed 332 pounds, ate beefsteak for breakfast, and would have been a load for even the most patriotic horses to pull. It must have been divine providence that the automobile became the official White House transportation for the Tafts.

Taft did not have to supply his own cars, but was given $25,000 by the government to buy automobiles for White House use. He spent the money on:

1 White Steamer
2 Pierce-Arrows
1 Baker Electric
2 motorcycle policemen
1 chauffeur

Metropolitan Policeman

Secret Service Agent

The presidential car went everywhere the president went—up the Mississippi River by boat, and across the plains by train—and the Secret Service went with him. On an outing they would follow his car on their motorcycles. The president would not allow Secret Service agents in the car with him.

The first motorcars looked very much like the old coaches, except that they were propelled by steam or gasoline and the wheels had pneumatic tires. The coachman's box became the chauffeur's seat, and the steering wheel replaced the reins and whip.

The Tafts' 1911 White Steamer was one of the last built before the manufacturer decided to concentrate on gasoline cars. It was virtually silent, had no fumes, and gave a smooth ride. But the Steamers were slow to start, and they declined in popularity with the coming of the self-starter in 1912.

1911 WHITE STEAMER MODEL M

40 horsepower engine
cost: $4,000
U.S. coat of arms on the doors
7-passenger touring model

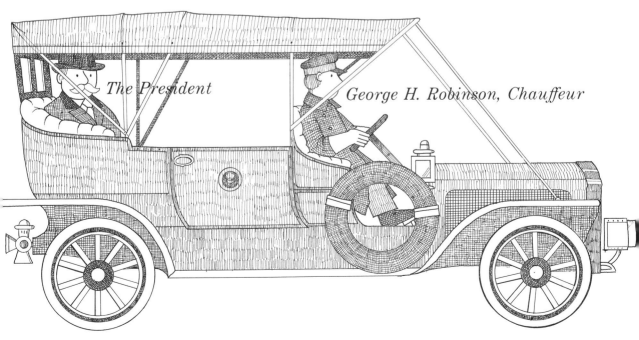

The President

George H. Robinson, Chauffeur

28th Woodrow Wilson, 1913–1921

During President Wilson's administration, the vehicle most frequently used was a 1916 Pierce-Arrow in which the president took a daily ride, going no faster than twenty-five miles per hour. The president would not allow a noisy motorcycle police escort, so instead he was followed by the Secret Service in their Cadillac. President Wilson liked the Pierce-Arrow so much that, after his term of office, he purchased the car for his personal use, presidential cars at this time being provided by the Secret Service.

The president of the United States drove in a large, powerful car, just as his predecessors generally rode in luxury coaches and carriages, as befitting their office. But now the scene across the country was changing. Long restricted to foot travel, public coaches, or train travel because he could not afford a costly carriage or expensive car, the ordinary citizen was suddenly emancipated by the introduction of Henry Ford's 1909 Model T. It was a bargain in those days at $825, and allowed the average person to travel just like the president of the United States—in a car.

1916 PIERCE-ARROW

Military Aide   *The President*

Mrs. Wilson

29th Warren G. Harding, 1921–1923

Ohio-born Warren G. Harding took his favorite car to Washington when he was elected president—a dashing 1920 Locomobile, a car he enjoyed driving himself. But he had to be content to be a passenger and ride in the back seat, for the Secret Service did not allow presidents to drive while in office.

The trusting Harding was not a good judge of people, and he surrounded himself with false friends. The scandals and corruption that ensued so hurt him politically and emotionally that he died after only two and a half years in office. His beloved Locomobile was shipped back to his home in Ohio by his wife, Florence.

1920 LOCOMOBILE

custom built 7-passenger model
gasoline powered 6-cylinder T-head engine
maximum speed 65 miles per hour

Edward P. White, Chauffeur

Mrs. Harding

Laddie Boy

The President

30th Calvin Coolidge, 1923–1929

When President Coolidge went for a drive around Washington in one of the five different Pierce-Arrows parked in the White House garage, he never allowed his chauffeur to go over sixteen miles per hour. Neither did he allow any other attention-getting noises like horn blowing or setting off the sirens. Frugal Yankee ways prevailed in his White House, even to the extent that the government would now rent cars from the auto manufacturers rather than purchasing them outright.

For presidential motorcades, the director of the Secret Service sat with the driver in the Coolidge car, followed by the Secret Service car with the White House physician, and then the press car.

Before the presidential car went on a motorcade, short trip, or just across town, the route was carefully checked by highly trained Secret Service agents to insure the safety of the president.

During Calvin Coolidge's administration, the White House garage contained more than eleven cars.

The Car

color: dark blue
White House insignia painted on door
silver eagle on radiator cap

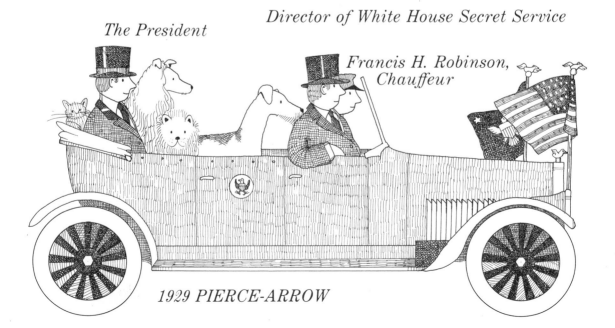

The President

Director of White House Secret Service

Francis H. Robinson,
Chauffeur

1929 PIERCE-ARROW

31st Herbert Hoover, 1929–1933

By 1929 every seventh person in the United States owned a car and was able to drive it on relatively smooth, paved roads. Disappearing slowly were the old roads made of wooden planks, wooden blocks, cobblestones, and bricks, and the unpaved country lanes where clouds of choking dust rose with each passing motor car. Even so, by 1950 more than half the roads were still unpaved.

During the Hoover administration the following cars were used:

White House Car no. 1
1 touring car
1 landaulet
2 Packards
1 1930 Cadillac limousine

There is no record today of the whereabouts of the handsome Cadillac limousine used by Herbert Hoover during his presidency.

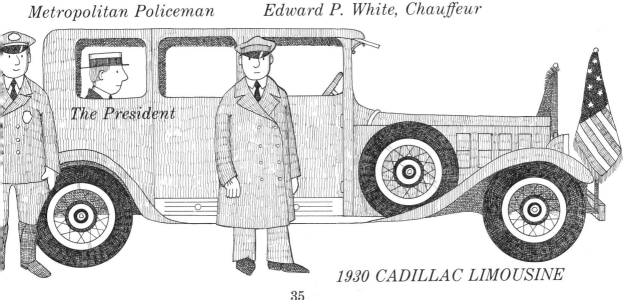

Metropolitan Policeman   *Edward P. White, Chauffeur*

The President

1930 CADILLAC LIMOUSINE

32nd Franklin D. Roosevelt, 1933–1945

President Roosevelt, the only man to be elected to office for four terms, and photographed thousands of times in many different automobiles during his twelve years in office, is best remembered in his favorite car, a 1939 Lincoln. Nicknamed "The Sunshine Special" because the president enjoyed riding with the top down in good weather, this car was driven 55,000 miles and used for eleven years.

Franklin Delano Roosevelt was a wartime president and world leader, which put an additional burden on the Secret Service in protecting him. On December 8, 1941, when President Roosevelt

1939 LINCOLN "SUNSHINE SPECIAL"

inch-thick bullet-resistant glass throughout car

Secret Service Agent

Secret Service Agent

The President's Son, John Roosevelt

The President

Mrs. Roosevelt

Fala

running board

went to Capitol Hill to address Congress about the Japanese invasion of Pearl Harbor, thirty-eight Secret Service agents surrounded him. During the long war which followed, he sailed to Casablanca and Yalta on a U.S. Navy vessel but left the presidential cars in the White House garage and used only military vehicles while abroad.

President Roosevelt persuaded the Secret Service to break a long-standing rule about presidents never driving, and drove a 1936 Ford Phaeton specially designed to accommodate his legs, paralyzed from polio.

President Roosevelt died during his fourth term of office and was succeeded by Vice-President Harry S Truman.

The Car

color: black with brown upholstery
weight: 9,300 pounds
wheelbase: 160 inches
length: 258 inches

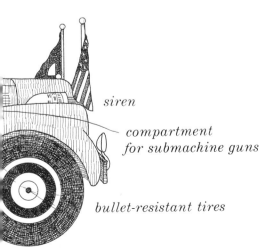

siren

compartment for submachine guns

bullet-resistant tires

33rd Harry S Truman, 1945–1953

In his inaugural parade, Harry S Truman rode in a Lincoln Cosmopolitan with Vice President elect Alben Barkley at his side and the men from Battery D, Kansas City, marching along beside the car. These were the soldiers from Captain Truman's World War I unit.

It was during the Truman years that the government started leasing cars from the Ford Motor Company, with an initial order of ten Lincoln Cosmopolitans. These cars had special features built in for the unique requirements of the president of the United States and his staff. The worldwide prestige of having the president ride in one of your company's cars cannot be overstated and far offset the nominal rental.

The Secret Service car, usually a convertible, was always driven directly behind the president's car and was filled with submachine guns.

Metropolitan Policeman

Any motorcycle police escorting the presidential car, other than on the White House grounds, were provided by the police force of the city or state where the motorcade occurred.

During the administration of President Truman, the Secret Service had grown to perform the following duties:

1. Protect the president and members of his immediate family
2. Protect the president-elect
3. Protect the vice-president
4. Catch counterfeiters
5. Detect and arrest criminals working against the Treasury Department laws
6. Supervise the White House police

THE SECRET SERVICE CAR

Secret Service Agents

Men from Battery D

The President-elect
The Vice President elect

1949 LINCOLN COSMOPOLITAN

34th Dwight D. Eisenhower, 1953–1961

By the time General Eisenhower, a World War II national hero, became president, there were thirty-six vehicles in service at the White House. President Eisenhower took one of them, a 1950 Lincoln, and had a bubbletop installed over the passenger section. This was a plastic bullet-resistant roof that gave protection to the president from bad weather and allowed people to see him. Eisenhower was a very popular man, and it had become an American custom that the president be visible to the public.

Other features of the specially built car were two comfortable folding seats in the rear passenger compartment, disappearing steps on either side of the rear fender for Secret Service men to stand on, and chrome handgrips on the sides of the car. The metal fixtures in the passenger section were gold-plated. There was a vanity case, a thermos bottle, writing desk, radio, and a shortwave radio for the Secret Service—and, of course, the now standard flashing red lights and warning siren up front by the fluttering American and presidential flags.

Secret Service Agents

Mrs. Eisenhower

The President

1950 LINCOLN "BUBBLETOP"

color: black with cherry red and black upholstery
weight: 6,450 pounds
wheelbase: 145 inches
length: 240 inches
high compression engine, V-type
152 horsepower
8 cylinders
heavy-duty Hydra-Matic transmission
two fresh-air heaters
armor-plating over engine, hood, and sides
bullet-resistant windows
leased from Ford Motor Company
headroom for high silk hats
bullet-resistant "bubbletop" plastic roof

35th John F. Kennedy, 1961–1963

John F. Kennedy rode through most of his administration in one of the most sumptuous cars ever to roll out of Detroit auto works. Four years on the drawing board at the Ford Motor Company, it was a dream car, a dark blue Lincoln with several interchangeable metal and plastic tops. The rear light and dark blue leather seats went up and down, there were two-way radio telephones, reading lights, and air conditioners, and carpet on the floor. The president could stand up and hold onto a handrail when the roof was off or slid back, or sit down under a lap robe embroidered with the presidential seal.

All of the Secret Service know-how gleaned from over sixty-two years of protecting the president went into the security features of the presidential limousine. There were handles and retractable foot stands for the Secret Service to use, and flashing red lights in the front bumper guards with the siren.

The car was nicknamed "Stretch" limousine, for a 1961 Lincoln Continental convertible had literally been sawed in half, and forty-one inches of steel plating were added to the middle section, "stretching" the vehicle to over twenty-one feet in length.

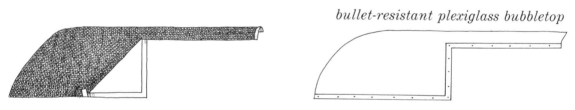

bullet-resistant plexiglass bubbletop

Interchangeable Tops Which Can Be Stored in Trunk of Car

The President *Mrs. Kennedy* *Secret Service Agen*

chrome

concealed handles

glass

John *Caroline*

retractable foot stand

chrome

President Kennedy was shot by an assassin in Dallas, Texas, on November 22, 1963, while riding in this car—the first time an American president was ever killed in a vehicle. A somewhat similar incident occurred in 1610 when Henry IV of France was stabbed to death in a coach by François Ravaillac while driving through a lane in Paris.

Shortly after the assassination in Dallas, the Kennedy limousine was shipped back to the Ford Motor Company by the Secret Service and completely rebuilt. It was transformed into the smoothest-running fortress on wheels, from its bullet-deflecting glass on top and sides to its rubber-coated aluminum bullet-resistant tires. This five-ton car, repainted black, became an awe-inspiring sight, protecting its new occupant, Lyndon B. Johnson, behind 1,600 pounds of steel plating and eight-pane-thick windows.

Over 130 limousines were in service at the White House during Kennedy's two years and ten months in office. The presidential limousine is now in the Henry Ford Museum in Dearborn, Michigan.

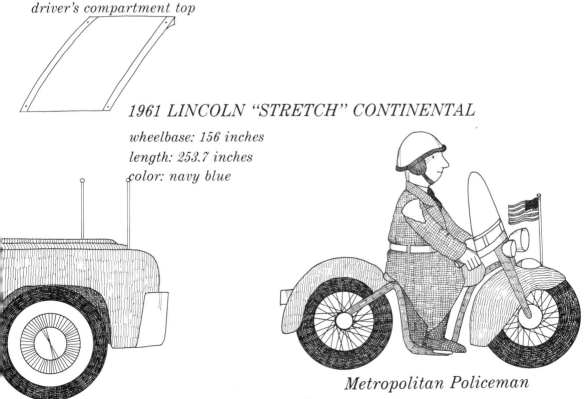

driver's compartment top

1961 LINCOLN "STRETCH" CONTINENTAL

wheelbase: 156 inches
length: 253.7 inches
color: navy blue

Metropolitan Policeman

36th Lyndon B. Johnson, 1963–1969

During the administration of President Johnson, many changes were made in the Secret Service as a result of the Kennedy assassination. Five hundred new agents were hired to protect the president and his family, both in and out of office. The White House Police, renamed the Executive Protection Service, employed 800 officers.

The beautiful blue limousine used by President Kennedy on the tragic day in Dallas, now a bullet-ridden horror, was shipped back to the Ford Motor Company in Dearborn, Michigan, to be completely rebuilt, leaving President Johnson without an official presidential limousine. The Ford Motor Company worked on the Kennedy limousine for one year and, after making major and extensive changes,

Metropolitan Policeman

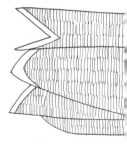

returned it to the White House for use by President Johnson. More than $1 million was spent on the rebuilding project.

During the year he was without an official presidential limousine, President Johnson had to find a suitably armored car for his use. He borrowed the steel-plated 1963 Cadillac limousine used by J. Edgar Hoover, the director of the F.B.I. This car was armored only in the body, but bullet-resistant glass was added right away for President Johnson.

President Johnson, known for his Great Society programs of government spending, did some about-face cost-cutting at the White House by getting rid of 111 official cars, leaving a total of 20. These did not include the Secret Service limousines and follow-ups.

1963 CADILLAC LIMOUSINE

armor-plating over engine, hood, and sides
bullet-resistant windows
leased from Ford Motor Company
bullet-resistant "bubbletop" plastic roof

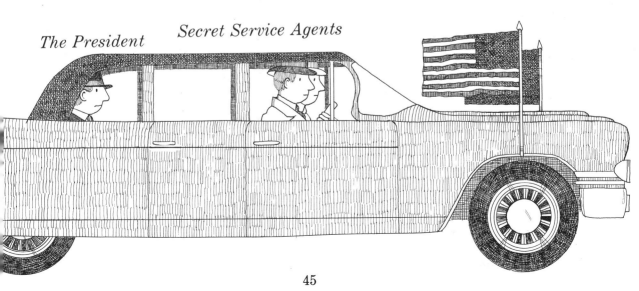

The President   *Secret Service Agents*

37th Richard M. Nixon, 1969-1974

Wearing special badges issued for use in a foreign country, Secret Service agents surround the presidential limousine. If the president wants to stand up and wave to the crowds, he tells his Secret Service driver, "I would like to stand up." The driver radios the car ahead and says, *"Potus*" would like to stand." The agents run back, pull down the bumper, and raise the handrail. Two agents always ride the back bumper when the president is standing in the car. The presidential car is flown all over the world with the president in Air Force planes and guarded night and day by Secret Service agents.

President Nixon used a 1968 Lincoln "Stretch" Continental limousine for official functions. It had the presidential seal on the middle

*Secret Service code word for president of the United States

bullet-resistant glass roof with vinyl cover   *Secret Service Agen*

Foreign Country Motorcycle Policeman

panel of the car. The roof was hinged to permit the president to stand in the rear compartment. There was a telephone and a sound system that allowed outside noises to be heard inside. The passenger compartment could hold six people. It was upholstered in silver-gray pinstripe cloth and vinyl trim and was carpeted in silver mouton. The American and presidential flags could be illuminated by three small spotlights mounted in each fender.

The Secret Service followed the Nixon limousine in sleek, black, custom-built convertibles bristling with handrails, footstands, and running boards. These steel-lined, armored cars were nicknamed "Queen Mary" and "Queen Elizabeth."

1968 LINCOLN "STRETCH" CONTINENTAL

wheelbase: 160 inches
length: 255 inches
color: black
fold-down bumper for Secret Service
handrails in rear for Secret Service

Mrs. Nixon

The President

foreign flag which replaces presidential flag outside United States

38th Gerald R. Ford, 1974–1977

The 1972 specially built Lincoln Continental presidential limousine was commissioned by the Secret Service and was two years in the making. Gerald Ford used it during his years in the White House when he succeeded the resigned Nixon.

A ride in this magnificent automobile must have been an unforgettable experience—sumptuous passenger section, aerospace-designed driver's compartment, super-powerful engine, and the lat-

The Car

color: black
wheelbase: 161 inches
length: 259 inches
width: 79.6 inches
height: 61.1 inches

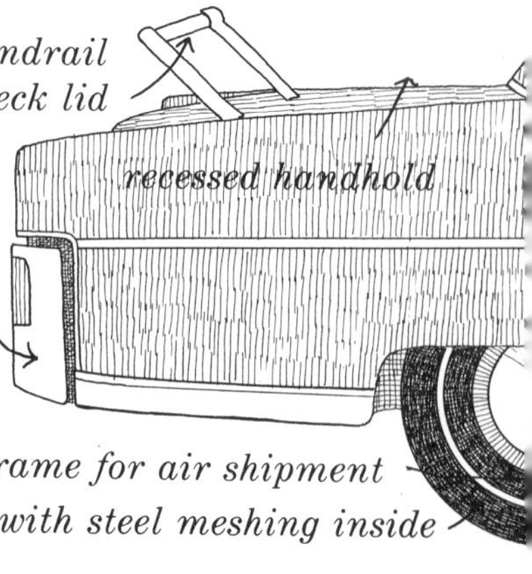

mechanically operated handrail
which disappears into deck lid

recessed handhold

rear bumper which folds down
into standing platform

special tie-down hooks welded under frame for air shipment
multiple security tires with steel meshing inside

est security and protection devices. The car represented the culmination of almost two hundred years of presidential travel that began when President Washington rattled through Philadelphia in a wooden coach with the four seasons delicately painted on the side panels.

This car, sometimes referred to as the "parade limo," was leased from the Ford Motor Company for $5,000 per year.

Interior

two-way communications system
powered sliding glass partition between compartments
medium gray leather seats and nylon carpet in 5-passenger compartment
fluorescent lights for reading and so passengers can be viewed from the outside
separate heating and air conditioning units for front and rear compartments
black leather seats and nylon carpet in driver's compartment

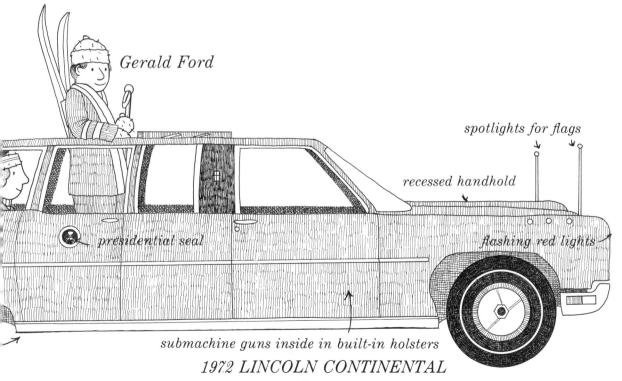

Gerald Ford

spotlights for flags

recessed handhold

presidential seal

flashing red lights

submachine guns inside in built-in holsters

1972 LINCOLN CONTINENTAL

39th Jimmy Carter, 1977–1981

The Carter presidential car, the 1972 Lincoln, is under the exclusive care and supervision of the Secret Service. Agents work with the automobile manufacturer in designing the luxury, safety, and security features of the presidential car; it is delivered from the factory to the Secret Service in Washington, D.C., who guard it night and day in the Secret Service garage. It is easier to get an appointment with the president of the United States than to set foot in that garage and look at the cars.

A motorcade of the thirty-ninth president of the United States is as impressive as the glittering chain of horses and carriages that accompanied the first president, George Washington, on official tours. A motorcade of flashing red lights and wailing sirens might go down Pennsylvania Avenue in this order:

1. Police car or motorcycles
2. The president of the United States
3. The Secret Service in their car, the "Batmobile"
4. High-level staff
5. The vice-president and his family
6. The Secret Service
7. The press
8. Communications

Secret Service Agents

Secret Service lapel pin

.357 magnum Smith & Wesson revolver

handcuffs on belt

extra bullets in belt pouch

Every moment the president is away from the White House, he is under constant guard by six or more Secret Service agents, and the background of every person who is with the president is carefully checked. Even the food the president eats is prepared under Secret Service supervision.

During Jimmy Carter's 1977 inaugural motorcade, the president decided to *get out of the car and walk!* The Secret Service rushed into position and formed a human square around the president and first lady as they strolled, hand in hand, on the brisk January day. A top White House aide explained, "The president likes to walk."

The President   *Mrs. Carter*   — *earphone*

wire to radio   *hidden mike up sleeve to radio*

radio under coat   *Secret Service Agent*

Speedloader

40th Ronald Reagan, 1981

Ronald Reagan's presidential limousine is the same one used by his predecessor and is referred to by the Secret Service as 200X. It has been completely refurbished and repainted four times since being put into use in 1974.

Seven years is a long time to have a car in service at the White House. It has been flown all over the world, securely chained in an Air Force plane. Its relegation to a museum should not be too far off. Already plans are on the drawing board for a new "stretch" limousine, but they are currently held up because of size and fuel consumption considerations.

The other presidential cars are a fleet of limousines known as "midnight Cadillacs"—silent, armored vehicles which wait through the dark and early dawn in the White House driveway—ready in case of emergency to evacuate the president and his family. But even this James Bond scenario has its flaw—the paint keeps falling off the escape cars.

Ronald Reagan

Secret Service Agents

1972 LINCOLN CONTINENTAL

Where to See
Presidential Carriages and Cars

George Washington	Mt. Vernon, Virginia Smithsonian Institution, Washington, D.C.
John Adams	None survive
Thomas Jefferson	Monticello, Virginia
James Madison	None survive
James Monroe	Shelburne Museum, Shelburne, Vermont
John Quincy Adams	None survive
Andrew Jackson	The Hermitage, Hermitage, Tennessee
Martin Van Buren	None survive
William Henry Harrison	None survive
John Tyler	None survive
James K. Polk	None survive
Zachary Taylor	None survive
Millard Fillmore	Buffalo and Erie County Historical Society, Buffalo, New York
Franklin Pierce	Private collection as of 1897
James Buchanan	Buchanan's home, "Wheatlands," Lancaster, Pennsylvania The Museum at Stony Brook, New York (not authenticated)
Abraham Lincoln	Studebaker Collection, Discovery Hall Museum, South Bend, Indiana; Chicago Historical Society, Chicago, Illinois; LaSalle County Historical Museum, Utica, Illinois
Andrew Johnson	None survive
Ulysses S. Grant	Smithsonian Institution, Washington, D.C. Studebaker Collection, Discovery Hall Museum, South Bend, Indiana
Rutherford B. Hayes	Rutherford B. Hayes Library, Fremont, Ohio
James A. Garfield	Lake County Historical Society, Mentor, Ohio (in storage)

Chester A. Arthur	Pikes Peak Ghost Town, Colorado Springs, Colorado
Grover Cleveland	Arbor Lodge State Historical Park, Nebraska City, Nebraska
Benjamin Harrison	Studebaker Collection, Discovery Hall Museum, South Bend, Indiana
William McKinley	Studebaker Collection, Discovery Hall Museum, South Bend, Indiana; Shelburne Museum, Shelburne, Vermont
Theodore Roosevelt	Henry Ford Museum, Dearborn, Michigan Smithsonian Institution, Washington, D.C.
William H. Taft	Henry Ford Museum, Dearborn, Michigan Heritage Plantation Car Museum, Sandwich, Massachusetts
Woodrow Wilson	Woodrow Wilson Birthplace Foundation, Staunton, Virginia
Warren G. Harding	Whereabouts unknown
Calvin Coolidge	Coolidge Homestead, Plymouth, Vermont
Herbert C. Hoover	Whereabouts unknown
Franklin D. Roosevelt	Franklin Delano Roosevelt Library, Hyde Park, New York; Henry Ford Museum, Dearborn, Michigan; Pikes Peak Ghost Town, Colorado Springs, Colorado; The State of New York Collection, New York State Museum, Albany, New York Private collections
Harry S Truman	Henry Ford Museum, Dearborn, Michigan Private collections Colorado Car Museum, Manitou Springs, Colorado
Dwight D. Eisenhower	Henry Ford Museum, Dearborn, Michigan Dwight D. Eisenhower Library, Abilene, Kansas
John F. Kennedy	Henry Ford Museum, Dearborn, Michigan Colorado Car Museum, Manitou Springs, Colorado

Lyndon B. Johnson	Henry Ford Museum, Dearborn, Michigan Colorado Car Museum, Manitou Springs, Colorado
Richard M. Nixon	Henry Ford Museum, Dearborn, Michigan Colorado Car Museum, Manitou Springs, Colorado
Gerald R. Ford	In use, or not available to the public
Jimmy Carter	In use, or not available to the public
Ronald Reagan	In use, or not available to the public

Glossary

Baker Electric	A motorcar powered by an electric engine.
Barouche	A four-wheeled, fair-weather carriage with a seat outside for the driver, facing seats inside for two couples, and a folding top over the back seat.
Brougham	A four-wheeled boxlike closed carriage for two or four persons, with the driver's seat outside. Named after the English statesman Lord Brougham.
Buggy	A light four-wheeled carriage with a single seat and a spring at right angles to the traveling direction.
Cabriolet	A light two-wheeled one-horse carriage with a folding top over the rear seat. For two people.
Carriage	A wheeled vehicle for conveying people, as one drawn by horses, and designed for comfort and elegance.
Chariot	A light four-wheeled pleasure carriage; any rather stately carriage.
Clarence Coach	A coach with a single upholstered seat across the back and a curved glass front. Below the curved glass and inside is a hinged seat for two people.
Coach	A large enclosed four-wheeled carriage.
Coachee	A six-passenger coach with the driver's seat inside. Used in the city and the country.
Coachman	The driver of a coach.
Cob	A thick-set horse with short legs and a high gait.
Crane neck	A design of eighteenth century carriages where two parallel iron rods under the carriage bend so the front wheels pass under them.
C Springs	Steel springs shaped like a C at the front and back of a carriage.
Elliptical Springs	Elliptically shaped metal springs.
Equipage	Carriage, horse, and attending servants.
Footman	A liveried servant who attends the door of a carriage and rides at the back.
Gig	A light two-wheeled one-horse carriage of the 1800's that uses C springs. Comfortable on poor roads.
Hammercloth	The cloth covering the driver's seat of a carriage.

Hammersmith	A metalworker in the carriage-making industry.
Jacobs Carriage	A carriage named after S. W. Jacobs, carriage maker of Philadelphia.
Joiner	A carpenter or carriage maker who constructs doors, windows, panels, and other interior woodwork.
Landau	A dignified four-wheeled open or closed carriage with a wide range of uses. Uses large, quiet horses. Top made in two parts that may be let down or folded back.
Landaulet	An automobile with an open driver's compartment and with a collapsible roof over the passenger section.
Limousine	A large, luxurious automobile.
Livery	The distinctive uniforms worn by coachmen and footmen.
Perch	A design of eighteenth century carriage making with a straight or slightly bent pole under the coach.
Phaeton	An inexpensive eighteenth century owner–driver carriage with a very high body. A two-wheeled vehicle and very dangerous to drive. Later four-wheeled carriages are also called phaetons.
Pleasure Wagon	A family wagon with movable seats to convert from family to farm use.
Postilion	One who rides on the left horse of the leaders when two or four horses are used to draw a carriage.
Rockaway	One of the most popular four-wheeled family carriages of the late nineteenth century, with a projecting roof over the driver and a fixed top on the carriage.
Speedloader	A set of six bullets which can be inserted in a gun all at once for quick reloading and firing.
Surrey	A small, light family vehicle with a removable top and drop sides. Seats four.
Undercarriage	The supporting framework of a vehicle.
Victoria	A low, light four-wheeled carriage for two with a folding top and a raised seat in front for the driver. Named after Queen Victoria.
Wheelwright	One who makes or repairs carriage wheels.

Bibliography

American Motorist, November 1970.

Augusta County Historical Society, The. "President Woodrow Wilson and His Pierce-Arrow." *The Augusta Historical Bulletin* 9, no. 1 (Spring 1973), pp. 44–57. Reprinted by the Woodrow Wilson Birthplace Foundation.

Baker, Lafayette Charles. *History of the United States Secret Service.* Philadelphia, 1869. Reprinted by AMS Press, 1973.

Collins, Herbert Ridgeway. *Presidents on Wheels.* Washington, D.C.: Acropolis Books, 1971.

Congressional Research Service 77–151G JK 516 #A5.

Congressional Research Service 77–161G JK 516 #A5, July 8, 1977.

Cooke, David C. *Your Treasury Department.* New York: W. W. Norton, 1964.

"Criminology and Police Science." *The Journal of Criminal Law* 47, No. 1, May–June 1956.

Ford Motor Co. News Releases.

Freidel, Frank. "Profiles of the Presidents," parts I–V. *The National Geographic,* November 1964, January 1965, May 1965, October 1965, January 1966.

Hyde, Wayne. *What Does a Secret Service Agent Do?* New York: Dodd, Mead & Co., 1962.

Landower Collection, New York Historical Society.

Nicholson, T. R. *Passenger Cars 1905–1912.* New York: Macmillan, 1971.

Roscoe, Theodore. *The Lincoln Assassination.* New York: Franklin Watts, 1971.

Tarr, László. *The History of the Carriage.* Translated by Elizabeth Hoch. New York: Arco Publishing Co., 1969.

Truman, Margaret. *White House Pets.* New York: David McKay Co., 1969.

U.S., Treasury Department, U.S. Secret Service.

The History of the United States Secret Service 1865–1975.